Power Up Your Job Search:

A Modern Approach to Interview Preparation

Gary W. Capone
and
Mark Henderson

Copyright 2009 Palladian International, LLC

All rights reserved. This book, or parts thereof, may not be reproduced in any form without the permission of the Palladian International, LLC. Exceptions are granted for brief excerpts used in published reviews.

Palladian International, LLC
105-A Lew Dewitt Blvd. Suite 197
Waynesboro, VA 22980

ISBN-13: 978-1-441-49153-4
ISBN-10: 1-44149-153-8

*This book is dedicated to
Melissa and Sandi
for their unwavering support
and encouragement.*

About the Authors

Gary W. Capone is Vice President and cofounder of Palladian International, LLC. He is a graduate of the Management and Technology Program at the University of Pennsylvania, where he concurrently earned a Bachelor's of Science in Mechanical Engineering and a Bachelor's of Science in Economics from the Wharton School of Business. Mr. Capone has experience in manufacturing, distribution, accounting, finance and human resources, gained from positions at PriceWaterhouseCoopers, Newell-Rubbermaid, Kforce, Raymond James and Target Corp. In 2006, he joined the Board of Directors of the Blue Ridge Chapter of APICS and in 2009 was elected Chapter President.

Mark Henderson is President and cofounder of Palladian International. He graduated with a Bachelor of Science degree from Norwich University and a Masters degree from Central Michigan University. He is also a graduate of the Defense Language School (Portuguese) and the US Army War College. Mr. Henderson served in the United States Army for 28 years, rising to the rank of Colonel. While in the Army, he had assignments in the Infantry, Transportation and Personnel, commanding units at the Company, Battalion and Brigade levels and served in locales around the globe. His military awards include the Defense Superior Service Medal, the Legion of Merit and the Order of St. Christopher. In 2002, Mark was selected as a Distinguished Member of the US Army Transportation Regiment. Mr. Henderson transitioned from the military to the corporate world, where he held positions of responsibility in Distribution, Operations and Transportation. He has served on the Greater Augusta County United Way Board of Directors, The Waynesboro Country Club Board of Directors, and is currently the President of the Atlantic Coast Collegiate Hockey League, comprising teams from UVA, Virginia Tech, Duke, UNC, Georgetown, and NC State.

Introduction

We started writing this book more than three years ago. The effort began with our desire to provide our candidates with a simple guide to help prepare them for an interview. At the time, we focused exclusively on executive recruiting.

Our firm, Palladian International, is a specialized executive recruiting firm, hired by corporations to find and attract the best talent. For us to be effective, it is important that the candidates we represent be able to communicate their potential effectively. This is where our interview guide got started.

We wanted a tool that would put all of our candidates in a position to communicate their skills, experiences and abilities honestly and effectively, enabling our clients to make the best assessment, and in turn, the best hiring decision. This was and still is important to us because few job seekers have ever been trained to interview. Many make basic mistakes that hurt their interview performance.

Our first interview guide was very short, around a dozen pages. Despite this, it was an extremely effective tool. There was no filler – every word of the guide added value.

Over time, we had a lot of candidates ask us for more. While the guide was very helpful, it only covered the most important elements of interviewing. We worked to develop a tool that would be much more comprehensive.

This book is the result of those efforts. We have stayed with the style of our original guide – short, concise and packed with value.

The Exercises

Reading a book is a great way to learn, but it does have some limitations. It is much easier to learn by doing. To help you get as much from this book as possible, we have a number of exercises designed to put our advice into practice.

The book is organized in a series of lessons – 26 in all. We have included exercises after each lesson. The activities are designed to be quick and easy to complete.

If you complete all of the exercises in the book, you will be far better prepared for your next interview than the vast majority of job seekers.

Try not to skip any of the exercises. Lessons and exercises at the beginning of the book form the basis for later lessons.

We hope you enjoy the book, and more importantly, improve your interview skills and performance.

Contents

About the Authors iv
Introduction v
Contents vii

Power Up 1
   THE INTERVIEWER 2
   THE COMPETITION 3
   INVEST IN YOURSELF 4

Lesson 1 The Interview Process 5
   THE PHONE SCREEN INTERVIEW 5
   A SECOND PHONE SCREEN INTERVIEW 6
   AN ON-SITE INTERVIEW 7
   A SECOND-ON SITE VISIT 8
   THE FINAL STEPS 8
   LESSON 1 EXERCISES 9

Lesson 2 Interview Structure 10
   TELL ME ABOUT YOURSELF 11
   QUESTIONS AND ANSWERS 12
   DO YOU HAVE ANY QUESTIONS? 13
   THE 10 STEPS IN THE INTERVIEW PREPARATION PROCESS: ... 14
   LESSON 2 EXERCISES 15

Lesson 3 What Is Important to an Employer? 17
   HOW DO YOU FIND OUT WHAT IS IMPORTANT TO A HIRING MANAGER? 17
   LESSON 3 EXERCISES 19

Lesson 4: Develop Your Positioning Statement 21
   TELL ME ABOUT YOURSELF 22
   WHY SHOULD I HIRE YOU? 23
   LESSON 4 EXERCISES 24

Lesson 5 Interview Types 26
   EXPERIENCE BASED 26
   BEHAVIOR BASED 27
   SKILL BASED 28
   CREATIVE/APTITUDE 28
   INTERVIEW TYPE MATRIX 29
   LESSON 5 EXERCISES 31

Lesson 6 Interview Style 32
   FRIENDLY 33
   CLINICAL 33
   CONFRONTATIONAL 34
   LESSON 6 EXERCISES 36

Lesson 7 Types of Interview Questions 37
TELL ME ABOUT YOURSELF 37
EXPERIENCE 38
TECHNICAL SKILLS 38
COMMUNICATIONS SKILLS 38
CAREER GOALS 38
BEHAVIOR BASED 38
COMPANY/INDUSTRY KNOWLEDGE 39
CAREER PROGRESSION 39
EDUCATION 39
APTITUDE 39
CREATIVE 39
COMPENSATION 39
OFF-LIMITS QUESTIONS 40
CONCLUSIONS 40
LESSON 7 EXERCISES 41

Lesson 8 STAR(L) 42
WHAT IS STAR(L) 43
THE ELEMENTS 43
LESSON 8 EXERCISES 45

Lesson 9 STAR(L) Example 46
LESSON 9 EXERCISES 50

Lesson 10 Experience Questions 51
CONFIDENTIALITY 53
LESSON 10 EXERCISES 55

Lesson 11 Skills Questions 56
LESSON 11 EXERCISES 59

Lesson 12 Communication Skills 60
LESSON 12 EXERCISES 62

Lesson 13 Career Goals 63
1. WORK ENVIRONMENT 64
2. WORK SCHEDULE 65
3. COMPANY CULTURE 65
4. RESPONSIBILITIES 65
5. LOCATION 66
6. COMPENSATION 66
7. PROGRESSION 67
LESSON 13 EXERCISES 68

Lesson 14 Behavior Based Questions 70
LESSON 14 EXERCISES 72

Lesson 15 Company and Industry Knowledge 73
LESSON 15 EXERCISES 75

Lesson 16 Career Progression 78
"I was fired." 79
"I had the opportunity to gain additional experience" 80
"I hated my job" 81
Lesson 16 Exercises 82

Lesson 17 Education 83
Recent Graduates 84
Lesson 17 Exercises 86

Lesson 18 Aptitude 87
Lesson 18 Exercises 89

Lesson 19 Creative 90
Lesson 19 Exercises 92

Lesson 20 Compensation 93
Lesson 20 Exercises 95

Lesson 21 Off Limits Questions 96

Lesson 22 Your Questions 98
Assessing Fit 98
The Future of the Company 99
Greatest Challenge 99
Biggest Obstacle 99

Lesson 23 Mock Interviews 102

Lesson 24 Going to Your Interview 106

Lesson 25 What to Expect 109
Settings 109
Interviewers 112

Lesson 26 After the Interview 114
Thank You Notes 114
Information Requests 115
Research the Company 115
Assess Your Performance 115

Conclusions 117
Continuous Improvement 118
Your Next Job Search 118
Final Thoughts 119

Appendix Interview Questions 120
Index 124

Power Up

A job interview is a critical element of your job search. It is the point in the hiring process where the company makes a hiring decision. Interviewing effectively is an essential skill. Unfortunately, many job seekers fail in this basic area.

We have screened and assessed thousands of candidates as executive recruiters. Every time we have a candidate interview with a client, we ask for feedback from both the candidate and the client after the interview. The assessment provided by the candidate is often very predictable. The job seeker almost always talks about how great the interview went. We estimate that more than 90% of the time, the candidate thinks they hit a home run.

We wish we had a 90% hire rate with candidates who go on interviews. The truth is that many of these interviews didn't go so well, and the job seeker has no idea why.

There are a number of reasons why a job seeker might overestimate their performance in an interview. First, many job seekers do not understand what a good interview looks like. Without a basis for comparison, they interpret their performance positively. The second reason is a candidate's inability to self-assess. Many people struggle with creating an objective image of their performance. Finally, job seekers often interpret the actions of an interviewer incorrectly.

The Interviewer

An interviewer may do several things that give the job seeker a positive impression, regardless of their actual performance.

Interviewers are generally very polite and courteous. They are trying to assess the job seeker. At this time, they want to sell the job seeker on the opportunity in case they decide to make an offer. The goal is to ensure that the candidate will accept an offer should one be extended.

This approach leads to compliments and positive comments about the job seeker. Usually, these comments mean little. The interviewer is just being polite. Job seekers, however, tend to respond to these statements and assume that they reflect an honest assessment of how the employer feels about them.

Interviewers will also avoid negative statements about the job seekers. They do this for two reasons. First, many are uncomfortable criticizing someone directly. Second, if the interviewer has made up their mind about something, they may not want to open a debate on the issue.

For example, picture a situation where the interviewer wants someone who is extremely strong in a particular technical area. During the interview, the job seeker reveals their experience in this area to be good but not exceptional. The interviewer decides the experience is not sufficient and intends to reject the candidate. Usually, an interviewer will avoid stating this to the candidate during the interview.

If the interviewer gives the job seeker their assessment of the technical skill, the candidate may disagree with the assessment. The job seeker will then try to argue their case and convince the hiring manager on their expertise. If the interviewer has made up their mind, discussing the candidate's expertise further is a waste of time for them. It is much easier to just avoid the discussion, and not give a specific negative feedback.

The Competition

Job seekers often fail to recognize the talent level of their competition. Most focus on their own ability to do a job. Being qualified for a position is the price of admission for an interview. Companies screen resumes to select only the most qualified individuals to interview.

Interviews are designed to further separate the best candidates from those that are qualified but not as strong. You can assume that your competition has a similar background to you. In fact, it is likely that some candidates are more qualified.

Being qualified will not get you hired. It may help you obtain an interview, but to receive an offer, you need to do much more.

The individual that is hired will be the person that offers the greatest value to the company. This is the ultimate purpose of an interview – to assess the potential contribution you will provide if you are hired.

Because most job seekers tend to focus on their qualifications, they do not present a clear picture of the value they will provide. They hope the interviewer will imagine their potential based on their qualifications. The problem with this is the interviewer will consider a number of candidates with a similar background. Why would an employer conclude your potential is higher than someone else with a similar background?

Invest In Yourself

It is common for a person to spend 12 years in school, followed by four years in college and then another year or two in a master's program. This can total 18 or more years of school and cost hundreds of thousands of dollars. Despite this, very few people invest time and effort in learning how to market themselves.

You have taken a great first step with this book. You will learn techniques to power up your interviewing skills and set yourself apart. The most important aspect is the recognition of your need to sell your potential in an interview.

Focus on the needs of the interviewer instead of simply facts about your background and you will make a much better impression and power up your next interview!

Lesson 1
The Interview Process

The Interview Process varies as much in style and approach as the people conducting the interviews. During this course, we will teach you how to identify and adapt to different interview styles. No matter what the style, the key fact remains, interviewing is the most important screening step for many companies. The following steps are typical:

The Phone Screen Interview

- An initial phone screen is typically a fact-finding call from the company to the job seeker. Most often, the call is from a representative of the company and is not from the primary decision maker for the position.

- The primary intent of a phone screen is to get clarification of details from your resume. This often focuses the conversation on details of your experience and your skills. The phone screen also starts the process of assessing whether your personality is a fit for their corporate environment.

- The goal of this phone interview is to determine whether to proceed with you as a candidate.

> When you are contacted, make sure the screening call will take place at a location and time of your choosing. You want to be relaxed and free from distractions. Make sure you respond with enthusiasm, and try to match the pace and tone of the interviewer. Maintain good posture and smile during the call. Many job seekers find standing during the call helps them relax.

A Second Phone Screen Interview

- If a company uses a second phone screen it is usually conducted by someone close to the hiring manager or on occasion, it may be done by the hiring manager.

- The intent of this call is to confirm that the positive things found in the initial phone screen are in line with the hiring manager's vision of the ideal candidate.

A phone screen is like an open book test. You can keep your interview notes in front of you during the call. Just make sure you avoid reading them verbatim – it is likely the interviewer will be able to tell you are reading.

An On-Site Interview

- When a company brings you on-site, they have already determined that you are very close to the type of candidate they want. During an on-site interview, you should assume that everyone you meet might have input as to whether you are hired or not. Be on your best behavior.

- You are typically going to interview with someone from Human Resources, someone from the department you are going to work in and the hiring manager. Sometimes you will also interview with the hiring manager's boss. Interviews may be conducted one-on-one, with multiple interviewers or in a group/panel format.

Pay close attention to the positives of the company... new technologies or equipment, sales growth, cost reduction and other successes. You can then mention these observations in subsequent interviews, or use the details to ask follow up questions.

- If you are interviewing at the site where you are potentially going to work, you will probably be given a tour. You may also be asked to complete some administrative paperwork, and you may be given some tests. Sometimes the paperwork and testing are done as a preliminary step to the on-site visit.

A Second-On Site Visit

- At lower levels, a second on-site visit is rare, but at more senior levels, additional on-site interviews are common. Companies conduct multiple face-to-face interviews so you can meet someone "higher up" in the company's structure. It may be the hiring manager's boss, a senior VP or even the CEO. This visit may mirror the first visit in style, or it may be less structured.

- The company's intent is to determine if you will be "a good fit" with the senior people you will be working with.

Some hiring managers will coach job seekers on how to interview with higher-level people. The reason for this is simple... the hiring manager has selected the job seeker as one of their final picks. If the candidate interviews poorly with senior management, it could refect poorly on the hiring manager. If a hiring manager gives you advice, listen but do not assume you are a shoe-in. You are probably not the only candidate still being considered.

The Final Steps

- Once a company has decided to hire you, you still have one more hurdle to pass--accepting an offer. Obviously, the company wants you. Ideally, you have used your on-site visit(s) to confirm that this is a company you want to join.

Lesson 1 Exercises

A key element of interviewing is demonstrating how you are the best candidate for the job. It is likely that you will be competing against other candidates that have a very similar background to you.

Write down a short description of what makes you different and better than others doing exactly the same job as you do.

_____

_____

_____

_____

Research the position you are pursuing. Try to gather as much information as you can about the expectations placed on individuals in this role. The more you understand how you will be assessed and evaluated, the more you can tailor your interview answers to these expectations.

Start by gathering a number of job descriptions for the position. Try to obtain these from different companies. A selection should give you a good idea of what is important to the company and hiring manager.

If possible, obtain a copy of an annual review from someone doing the job you are pursuing. If you already had a similar role, your last annual review will work. If not, ask someone in a role similar to the position you seek to share their annual review with you.

We are going to use this information in Lesson 3.

Lesson 2
Interview Structure

Every interview will include three main segments. The format and structure for the interview can vary greatly. In fact, the style of an interview can change during the interview. Despite this, these three segments will be found in most interviews:

- The interview begins with the introduction between you and the interviewer. This introduction will usually take the form of "Tell Me About Yourself."

- Next, you move on to the Questions and Answers portion of the interview, where you provide more insight into who you are, and what you bring to the table.

- Finally, the interview will conclude with your opportunity to ask some questions. This is where you start forming an idea of whether the job, the company and the environment are right for you.

Preparing for all three sections of the interview is necessary for you to present yourself in the best possible light. Understanding these three areas is your first step in preparing.

Tell Me About Yourself

The start of every interview is the most critical part of the interview. Most interviewers start by asking a seemingly easy question to put you at ease and to kick things off. This question is "Tell Me About Yourself." Failing to answer this successfully can doom an interview. Fortunately, it is an easy question to answer and the only question you know you will be asked, so you can prepare for it.

The key to this question is being brief and articulate. You control the information you provide and you control how long you talk. You will want to talk about your background and summarize it clearly. This provides the interviewer with an insight into why you are qualified for the position. Equally important, it demonstrates your communication skills.

To be successful here, avoid following the <u>exact</u> structure of your resume. Your goal is to get the interviewer excited about talking to you. Your resume has already been reviewed, so use this time to describe yourself in "strategic terms." You want to demonstrate your background and abilities clearly, but also try to give some insight into one or all of four fundamental issues EVERY company wants to know:

- What have you done that has caused you to stand out among your peers?

- What have you done to cause your company to increase revenues, improve market share or add to the company's growth?

- What have you done that ever caused your company to reduce costs?

- What have you done that ever caused your company to save time or to become more efficient?

The challenge is trying to articulate all of this in a tight, precise and exciting package. Your goal is to do this in two to four minutes. We are going to work on your positioning statement and Tell Me About Yourself answer in Lesson 4. These elements are extremely important and will provide the foundation for much of the course.

One of the common difficulties we see job seekers struggle with is identifying their accomplishments and contributions. Many people initially respond to the four questions by answering "Nothing." When we dig deeper, we can often find several examples of how the job seeker has contributed to the growth, cost cutting and efficiency improvements of the company. If you do not think of examples to answer these questions, stick with it until you do, or get help from an interview coach who will work with you to identify your contributions.

Questions and Answers

The questions and answers portion of the interview will be the most time consuming portion of the interview. This is the time when the interviewer will ask you a series of questions and listen to your answers. It can become a back and forth dialog, but is typically a question from the interviewer, followed by your answer, then another question from the interviewer and so on. Most interviewers will spend twenty to thirty minutes in this phase, although it can be shorter or longer. There are cases when these sessions can last significantly longer.

You need to prepare a variety of stories from your background and make sure you know them inside and out. This may seem easy, but for many of us, remembering the details of our career from ten or more years ago does not just happen. Ideally, you want five to ten stories that demonstrate your abilities very clearly. You will then use these to answer whichever question is asked. By rehearsing these stories, you will be able to adapt them to highlight your various skills and abilities. We will start developing these stories in Lesson 8 where we introduce a very powerful technique that will help structure your interview answers.

The more specific the examples you provide in your answers, the more effective you will be. Showing clearly what you have done in the past is a great way to build credibility and stand out from your competition.

Do You Have Any Questions?

The final portion of the interview will be your opportunity to ask questions. You should always have questions to ask. This is your opportunity to learn more about the company and the position. Remember that in an interview, one objective is to get the job and an equally important objective is to determine whether you want the job. Ask questions that will help further your understanding of the opportunity, while continuing to project an image of the professional, intelligent candidate that you are.

Do not try to think of questions to ask during the interview. You need to prepare ahead of time. Develop a few questions you can ask. You do not have to ask any of the questions you prepare, but you will be ready and will not get caught without a question to ask.

The 10 Steps in the Interview Preparation Process:

Preparing to interview requires successfully completing 10 steps. This course will cover all these ten steps in detail:

1. *Assess your strengths, abilities, skills and accomplishments*
2. *Research the skills and abilities required for the position you are pursuing*
3. *Develop your positioning statement*
4. *Assess your interview skills*
5. *Work on developing stories and answers that you can use during the interview*
6. *Practice your interview skills*
7. *Research the company to develop questions to ask*
8. *Conduct mock interviews*
9. *Get organized to go to the interview*
10. *Go and ace the interview!*

This ten-step process will guide you as you improve your interview skills. Some of the steps can be covered in a single lesson, while others will require multiple lessons to master.

The first step is to assess yourself. To be successful at interviewing, it is essential that you be able to communicate why you are someone that a company should want to hire.

Lesson 2 Exercises

1.   Describe your accomplishments over the last five years.

2.   What makes you different from others in your field who are doing exactly the same job as you?

3.   Describe the skills that make you stand out in your industry.

4. *What talents and abilities do you possess that relate to your career?*

_____

_____

_____

_____

Lesson 3
What Is Important to an Employer?

It is essential that you demonstrate your ability to be successful in the role you are seeking. The interviewer will strive to assess your potential. You can make the process go smoother, and improve your chances, by anticipating the criteria they will use to evaluate you.

How do you find out what is important to a hiring manager?

If you are already doing a job similar to the one you are pursuing, look at your most recent annual review. There is a good chance the expectations of this position will be the same from one company to another. What may change is the relative importance of those expectations. A minor focus of a position at one company might be the primary focus of the same position at another company.

If you are making a change into a different role, you will need to do more research. You can either find someone in the role you are pursuing or research job postings on the Internet. Talking to someone in the role you are pursuing is a great way to understand the position's requirements. You can also read job descriptions published by other companies to see what they require.

You can also gain insight into the priorities of the position from the strategy of the company. The mission statement, website and press releases of a company will help you understand the goals of the company. You can prioritize the responsibilities of the position based on how they would support the overall corporate strategy.

No matter how you gather the information, you are wise to develop a profile of the skills, abilities and experiences that are important to the hiring manager for the position.

By looking at numerous positions, from different employers, you will get a better picture of what criteria is essential. It is possible that a hiring manager will want a certain skill or ability but may forget to write it into the job description. It is far less likely that every hiring manager at every company will overlook the same critical skill. By reviewing several similar job descriptions, you gain a clearer picture.

| LinkedIn is a great resource for researching jobs and companies. You can post a question to Linkedin Answers about the career field or job that you are pursuing. You can also identify people working in that job and connect directly with them. (www.linkedin.com) |

Lesson 3 Exercises

1. *Examine the annual review you obtained after Lesson 1. What are the basic expectations for the position? What are the expectations for the position that separate an average performance from an exceptional one?*

2. *Talk to someone you work with now in the role you are pursuing. Ask them what skills and abilities make them successful. Ask them what background someone needs to move into the position.*

3. *Research similar job descriptions. Go to a job board or two and search for the position you are seeking. Do not screen on geography since you are simply doing research. Once you find an appropriate position, look at the requirements. Copy these into a document and move on to the next description. Keep doing this until you have saved a list of requirements from at least ten postings.*

4. *Benchmark the Data. Compile all the requirements from the annual reviews, your discussions with people in the field and job description research. Are there any skills that consistently appear throughout your research? Are there skills that some companies emphasize strongly, and others fail to mention? List the top skills found in your research:*

- _____
- _____
- _____
- _____
- _____
- _____
- _____
- _____

Lesson 4: Develop Your Positioning Statement

An elevator speech is a short script that gives your background. It is designed to be short, usually under a minute. The idea is based on taking advantage of a chance meeting in an elevator. You get into an elevator with a person you do not know. You exchange greetings and each might happen to ask what the other one does. You only have a short time to answer, so you quickly convey the key points of your career.

Although having a good elevator speech will help your networking efforts, it serves a more important purpose. It provides the basic positioning statement that you are going to use throughout your career search. In your job search, and in every interview, you need to market and sell yourself. This requires creating an impression of what you have done, and what you are capable of doing. Your elevator speech, or positioning statement, will summarize your potential value to an employer.

Once you have developed your 30-60 second positioning statement, you can start using it in your search. This is usually a good foundation for a cover letter. Some people place their positioning statement at the top of their resume as an executive summary or professional profile.

Your positioning statement will also serve as the basis of your answer to the most common interview question – "Tell Me About Yourself."

Tell Me About Yourself

In Lesson 1, we discussed the structure of an interview. It is common for an interview to start with a broad question about your background... something similar to "Tell Me About Yourself." The interview will then move into a question and answer phase, and conclude with the job seeker asking questions of the interviewer.

Making a good impression with your "Tell Me About Yourself" answer is critical. This kicks off the interview.

Once you have your positioning statement, you will need to expand it for use here. In Lesson 2, you researched the key skills and abilities you need for the position. Now, describe your experience with each skill in the "Tell Me About Yourself" answer. This gives you the opportunity to make a very strong case for yourself at the very beginning of the interview.

The other topic you should cover is your motivation throughout your career. Your resume probably does not show why you made certain career moves. Describing the transitions in your resume, instead of the details of each position, is a useful technique.

Your answer to this question should be 2-5 minutes long, with 3-4 minutes being ideal. Because you know you are going to get this question in most interviews, it is the one question you can prepare a specific answer to, ahead of time.

Why Should I Hire You?

You may run into a general question asking for an overall assessment of yourself. There are a number of ways it might present itself:

- Why should I hire you?
- What makes you better than others doing your job?
- Why do you think you will be successful here?

The elevator speech and "Tell Me About Yourself" answer will provide the basis for answering these questions. At its core, your positioning statement summarizes your primary value to an employer.

> Your positioning statement and "Tell me about yourself" answer should focus on your professional career. Personal information should not be included. Although a rarity, there are interviewers that want to learn about your personality and interests outside of work. If this is the goal of the interviewer, they will ask a follow up question focused on your interests. You should then shift gears and provide some background on your interests and hobbies.

Lesson 4 Exercises

1. *Write your positioning statement. This should be 30 seconds long and explain the most important aspect of your career.*

2. *Write your "Tell Me About Yourself" answer. Script your answer for this question. Highlight your accomplishments and experience with the skills that are critical to the position and explain your progression between positions. This should be 3-4 minutes long.*

   INTRO *(A variation of your positioning statement):*

   BODY

CONCLUSION:

3. *Practice: Deliver your "Tell Me About Yourself" answer several times. Time yourself to see if you are in the 3-4 minute range.*
4. *Once you are comfortable with your answer, ask someone to listen to you and get their impression. This person could be a friend or coworker. Ideally, they understand the position you are pursuing and will give you honest feedback.*

Lesson 5
Interview Types

There are four primary types of interviews – Experience Based, Behavior Based, Skill Based, and Creative/Aptitude Based interviews. Understanding what to expect with each type will help you to adapt to every interviewer.

Experience Based

An experience based interview reviews your experiences, typically in the order they are presented on your resume. Some experience based interviews simply follow your resume exactly. The interviewer asks you to describe each position and some of the details of the position.

Experience based interviews typically generate a good dialog between the job seeker and the interviewer, with lots of follow up questions.

Although these interviews may seem like a cakewalk, there is one major pitfall. By utilizing your resume as the guide for which questions they ask, the interviewer is not sharing their decision-making criteria with you. It is possible that an important requirement will be skipped because your resume does not mention it.

This is why it is essential to understand fully the position you are seeking. Be prepared to demonstrate that you meet each requirement and can succeed in the role. That way, you can volunteer information about skills or abilities that might not be prominent on your resume, but are important to the interviewer.

Experience Based Example Question: "At ABC Company, how many people did you manage and what were your responsibilities?"

Behavior Based

A behavior based interview uses situation based questions designed to solicit examples of your performance. These interviews tend to be structured, with a pre-scripted set of questions. The interviewer will have specific criteria in mind that they will assess throughout the interview.

The common format for behavior based questions is "Tell me about a time when you…" The questions direct you to describe a specific situation in your background. Some of the situations may be major milestones in your career; others may be routine, day-to-day activities.

It is important to be able to articulate your accomplishments in a variety of areas to be successful with this type of interview. Because the interviewer is asking you to describe situations, it is not sufficient to say you have experience with something. You have to be able to show what you did.

Behavior Based Example Question: "Tell me about a time when you faced a difficult leadership challenge."

Skill Based

Skill based interviews focus on assessing specific technical skills. This type of interview is most common in IT and engineering positions, but is also conducted in other fields.

The goal of the skill based interview is to verify your skill level. This type of interview is often conducted by a technical expert within an organization. To be successful in this type of interview, you need to be knowledgeable and have the ability to articulate your answers. It can be helpful to provide specific examples of what you have done with a particular skill.

Skill Based Example Question: "Give me a few examples of macros you have written in Excel."

Creative/Aptitude

A creative or aptitude interview is designed to assess your potential. Often the questions have no right or wrong answer. What is most important is how you arrived at your answer.

This type of interview is found in fields requiring high intelligence and exceptional creativity. Advertising agencies, design firms, and software developers are some of the types of companies that may interview this way.

The most important thing to do in an interview like this is to stay relaxed. Your thought process is being assessed, so think through your answers. Often, it is extremely difficult to anticipate what answer the interviewer is looking for, if they even have an answer in mind. As a result, it is much better to just be yourself and go with your gut.

Creative Based Example Question: "If you were a tree, what kind of tree would you be?"

Interview Type Matrix

Position Example	Experience Based	Behavior Based	Skill Based	Creative / Aptitude
Finance / Accounting	Very Common	Rare	Very Common	Rare
Leadership / Management	Common	Very Common	Rare	Rare
Healthcare	Common	Common	Common	Rare
Engineering / Scientific	Common	Rare	Very Common	Rare
Management Consulting	Common	Common	Common	Common
IT	Common	Rare	Very Common	Common
Construction	Very Common	Rare	Common	Rare
Design	Common	Rare	Common	Very Common
Sales	Common	Common	Rare	Rare

Preparing for the four types of interviews will help you adapt to any situation. It is rare to find an interviewer that adheres to a single type for the duration of the interview. Most will include questions from several or all of the types. To be successful, you need to be flexible and prepared. By working on all four types, it is less likely that you will be caught off guard or surprised in an interview.

Lesson 5 Exercises

1. What interview types should you expect in your career field?

   _____
   _____
   _____
   _____
   _____

2. Which interview types are strengths for you? Which are weaknesses?

   _____
   _____
   _____
   _____
   _____

Lesson 6
Interview Style

The personality and style of the interviewer will play a significant factor in an interview. One or two styles may feel very natural for you, while the others may be very uncomfortable. It is important to adapt to your interviewer. More significant to your success, you must remain confident regardless of the style of the interviewer.

This can be difficult for many job seekers who may interpret the style of the interviewer as an indication of how they are being assessed. A friendly, outgoing interviewer often leads job seekers to think they have done very well, while a clinical or confrontational interviewer may do the opposite. The truth could be vastly different.

Friendly

An interviewer with a friendly style will foster a dialog and work to uncover the personality of the candidate. The interview evolves into something that is much more of a conversation.

Do not let the friendly exchange give you the impression that you do not have to sell yourself. This style is most often the result of the personality of the interviewer, not a reflection of their opinion of you. This makes it important to stay focused on demonstrating your abilities and potential.

It is common for interviewers to adopt a friendly style over lunch, during facility tours and other situations outside of the office. Stay professional regardless of the situation. We have watched job seekers do great in a series of interviews and then drop their professionalism at lunch, thereby sabotaging their chances.

Clinical

In a clinical interview, the interviewer strives to remain emotionless throughout the interview. The interviewer does this to reduce the influence of their personality on your presentation.

The challenge with this style is that the job seeker never gets any feedback from the interviewer. The interview feels more like a performance than a conversation.

The key to being effective in this style of interview is to stay focused on telling your story. Many job seekers find this style distracting or intimidating. One pitfall many encounter is wondering how to conclude an answer. If the interviewer asks an open-ended question, it can be difficult to know that you have covered everything you should.

An open-ended question requires a descriptive answer, in contrast to a closed-ended question that has a short, definitive answer. Open-ended questions often start with "describe," "tell me about" or "how do you feel about." The challenge with open-ended questions is knowing when you have adequately answered.

Some job seekers end up rambling and repeating information. They are craving some body language or acknowledgement to hint or confirm that they have answered the question. Unfortunately, the interviewer remains stone-faced waiting for the job seeker to indicate they are done.

You will not receive immediate feedback from the interviewer. They will remain emotionless. You cannot infer from this whether your interview performance was good or bad. Do not let doubts creep in – confidence is extremely important. With this style interview, you have no way of knowing how you are doing, so stay positive and upbeat. This will improve your chances.

Confrontational

A confrontational interview is the least common style, but often the most difficult. With this style, the interviewer strives to make the candidate uncomfortable in an effort to assess the job seeker's ability to handle adversity and confrontation.

To put pressure on the job seeker, the interview may ask the same or similar questions multiple times, often challenging the candidate's answer. The goal is to uncover a weakness and attack it.

> The core of this style focuses on the weaknesses and failures of the job seeker. A good way to handle this is to discuss what you learned from your failures. Everyone has failed. Successful candidates demonstrate how they have grown from failures so they will not repeat them.

If you end up in an interview like this, staying calm is critical. Do not take the confrontation and criticism personally. Stay focused on your abilities. If the interviewer focuses on your weaknesses, make sure you can discuss how you compensate so that the weaknesses do not hurt your performance.

Finally, assess, for yourself, whether the interviewer's style is a reflection of the corporate culture, or just that individual.

Lesson 6 Exercises

1. *What interview styles have you encountered in the past?*

   _____

   _____

   _____

   _____

   _____

2. *What interview styles are your strengths or weaknesses? Would any of the styles affect the impression you make in an interview?*

   _____

   _____

   _____

   _____

   _____

Lesson 7
Types of Interview Questions

The number of potential interview questions you might face is virtually unlimited. It may seem impossible to prepare for all of them. It is impossible - without the right strategy.

Fortunately, breaking down the questions into specific categories will allow you to prepare for some of the more common interview questions. It will also prepare you to adapt to unexpected questions successfully.

Tell Me About Yourself

Most interviews start with an icebreaker question that will ask you to summarize your background. This question is so prevalent and important that we focused on it in Lesson 3. You should have a strong "Tell Me About Yourself" answer prepared at this point. If you do not, go back to Lesson 3 and work on it. If you are unsure of your answer, schedule a one-on-one coaching session with a Palladian interview coach, and we will help you fine-tune your answer.

Experience

Many interviewers will focus on your professional experience. These questions will ask you to explain details of the jobs you have held.

Technical Skills

Interviews for technical positions will often have a lot of skill based questions. Questions about your skills may not be limited to technical positions. Most interviews will look at your skills even in less technical roles.

Communications Skills

Every interview is, at its core, an assessment of your communication skills. You may be asked directly about your ability to communicate effectively, or the interviewer may evaluate your communications skills indirectly. Either way, your communications skills will be assessed.

Career Goals

You need to know your goals and objectives. Many interviewers want to know the direction you are trying to drive your career.

Behavior Based

Behavior based questions focus on asking you to describe a specific situation from your experience and how you acted in that situation. These questions are similar to the experience and skill questions.

Company/Industry Knowledge

You are expected to research a company and industry before interviewing. Some interviewers will test this by asking specific questions that they feel you should be able to answer fully.

Career Progression

Most interviewers will ask for details of why you made specific career changes.

Education

You can expect both formal and informal questions about your education. Recent college graduates will see more of these questions.

Aptitude

Some interviewers will ask questions designed to test your aptitude and reasoning ability. Usually, you will see this in the form of an assessment test, but it may also be addressed in the interview.

Creative

Highly creative fields may focus the interview on assessing your creative ability and talents.

Compensation

At some point in the interview process, the discussion of money, benefits and other compensation factors will come up.

Off-Limits Questions

There are a variety of questions that interviewers should not ask. These questions focus on race, age, religion, sexual orientation, family status and other factors.

Conclusions

It is important to review and prepare for each category of questions you may encounter in an interview.

If you develop a clear picture of yourself for each category, you should be able to adapt your information to any question. We will work on each category in detail in future lessons.

Lesson 7 Exercises

Practice your Tell Me About Yourself answer. We cannot emphasize enough how important this is. You can expect some version of this in every interview, and you need to be prepared.

Tell Me About Yourself Checklist:

- *Is your answer 3-4 minutes long?*
- *Do you highlight your positioning statement?*
- *Do you back up your positioning statement with specific accomplishments that demonstrate your prior success?*
- *Do you explain any major career transitions or gaps in your career path? (it's often better to hit these head on and explain them early in the process)*
- *Do you highlight key skills relevant to the position you are seeking and demonstrate your proficiency with an accomplishment that shows you were successful with each skill? (you don't need to discuss every skill needed for the position, but should hit on the top skills. You may limit this to one skill, or talk about two or three).*

Lesson 8
STAR(L)

In Lesson 7, we promised to teach how to adapt to unforeseen interview questions – questions that could completely blindside you in an interview. To do this, we are going to cover one of the most powerful techniques in this course – ***The STAR(L).***

The technique relies on preparing powerful stories from your experience. You are going to learn a way to prepare answers to questions without having to predict what questions you will be asked. This technique will help you outperform your competition.

The technique is the STAR(L). This technique is also called PAR, and there are other acronyms for it. The acronym is not what is important; the structure is the key. We are going to review the basics of the technique in this lesson and explain how to apply this technique in future lessons.

What Is STAR(L)

STAR(L) stands for **Situation, Thoughts, Actions and Results**. The L is for **Lessons Learned**. If you answer a question in this format, it will make it very easy for the interviewer to follow what you say. It will also help you stay on topic and give you a clearly defined conclusion to your answer. We have all had times in interviews where we have been surprised by a question and end up rambling on some tangent. This can be avoided by using the STAR(L) method.

The Elements

- **Situation** – Describe the situation that you are going to discuss. This should be an overview of the challenge or obstacle you met. It should also provide the transition from the question that you are answering to the story that you are going to tell.

- **Thoughts** – Discuss your thoughts on the situation. What concerns and issues did you have? How did you approach and analyze the situation? Finally, what plans did you make?

- **Actions** – What actions did you take?

- **Results** – What were the results of your actions?

- **Lessons Learned** – If applicable, what did you take away from the experience that will help you in the future?

Do not overlook the Lessons Learned section. Discussing how you have developed as a professional will set you apart from the vast majority of your competition. Very few people do this and it can help you hit a home run.

Utilizing the STAR(L) format in an interview will keep you on task and make it very easy for the interviewer to follow your answer. You may spend several minutes answering a question, but you are basically breaking it down into 30-second pieces. This keeps your interviewer interested and keeps you focused on the question. The approach also demonstrates your analytical ability since it follows a common problem solving approach:

- Define the Problem
- Plan a Solution
- Implement the Solution
- Measure the Results

Bottom line: It is inevitable that you will be required to think on your feet during an interview. However, framing your response using the STAR(L) Method will result in more effective answers.

Lesson 8 Exercises

Develop three STAR(L) stories that demonstrate your effectiveness. These stories should answer questions such as:

- *Tell me about a time when you had to work under a tight deadline.*

- *What accomplishment are you most proud of?*

- *Tell me about a project you managed.*

Lesson 9
STAR(L) Example

The STAR(L) method is a very powerful technique that will help you prepare for an interview and structure your interview answers. We are going to cover an example showing a typical answer and a STAR(L) answer to the same question.

A common interview question is "What is your greatest strength?" A typical answer looks something like this:

> *"My greatest strength is that I am highly organized. I have always been well organized, and have continued to refine this skill throughout my career. I build daily, weekly and monthly plans, and track my performance to these plans so that I stay on task and successfully accomplish every project I work on."*

This would be a pretty good answer – better than many we see. It clearly answers the question and is specific about what the strength is and how you apply the strength. Although the response above would be acceptable in most interviews, putting the same answer into the STAR(L) Model will turn a "pretty good" answer into a home run. Here's what the STAR(L) answer might look like:

> *"My greatest strength is that I am highly organized. I have worked on a variety of large projects in my career that have required great attention to detail. One of the most challenging was the roll-out of new product. I was the project manager for the roll-out and had to coordinate the work of the engineering, production, sales, marketing and accounting departments to ensure a successful roll-out. Making it even more challenging, we had the goal to complete the roll-out in three months, two months faster the last year's roll-out. I knew that being organized was going to be the key to success. I also knew that I would have to communicate with everyone to keep them in the game with me. Additionally, I recognized there were some people that could probably give me some great advice. To get the project rolling, I first identified the key players I was going to have to work with. I then met with each of them individually to develop their buy-in and cooperation. I scheduled a project meeting with all of them, where we assigned responsibilities and set the roll-out schedule. I used this roll-out schedule to hold everyone accountable and communicated with each project member, in person and by email, on a daily basis to ensure that we did not fall behind. This required reviewing every task on the project. I also sought out the advice of another manager. Based on his recommendation, I utilized Microsoft Project to track all the details. This was the first time I had used this software and I found that it really made the management of the project much easier and more successful. My organization skills were critical in keeping everything straight. By communicating with everyone up front and managing the details very closely, we successfully rolled-out the product a week ahead of schedule. Although I felt very*

successful with this project, I learned a number of project management techniques using MS Project. In the future, I'm confident I could accomplish a similar project faster and with fewer issues."

Looking at the STAR (L) response, here is how it broke down:

Intro:	My greatest strength is that I am highly organized. I have worked on a variety of large projects in my career that have required great attention to detail.
Situation:	One of the most challenging was the roll-out of new product. I was the project manager for the roll-out and had to coordinate the work of the engineering, production, sales, marketing and accounting departments to ensure a successful roll-out. Making it even more challenging, we had the goal to complete the rollout in three months, two months faster the last year's rollout.
Thoughts:	I knew that being organized was going to be the key to success. I also knew that I would have to communicate with everyone to keep them in the game with me. Additionally, I recognized there were some people that could probably give me some great advice.
Actions:	To get the project rolling, I first identified the key players I was going to have to work with. I then met with each of them individually to develop their buy-in and cooperation. I scheduled a project meeting with all of them, where we assigned responsibilities and set the rollout schedule. I used this roll-out schedule to hold everyone accountable and communicated with each project member, in person and by email, on a daily basis to ensure that we did not fall behind. This required reviewing every task on the project. I also sought out the advice of another manager. Based on his

	recommendation, I utilized Microsoft Project to track all the details. This was the first time I had used this software and I found that it really made the management of the project much easier and more successful.
Results:	My organization skills were critical in keeping everything straight. By communicating with everyone up front and managing the details very closely, we successfully rolled-out the product a week ahead of schedule.
Lessons Learned:	Although I felt very successful with this project, I learned a number of project management techniques using MS Project. In the future, I'm confident I could accomplish a similar project faster and with fewer issues."

The STAR(L) method of answering a question is an extremely powerful and effective technique. By providing an example as you answer a question, you show the interviewer what you are capable of doing.

In addition, utilizing a logical sequence that is easy to follow will make a great impression. Many job seekers find it difficult to communicate complicated answers in a simple way. Either they jump around in a confusing way, or they ramble on-and-on. The STAR(L) will help keep you on track.

The STAR(L) method is most effective when you prepare ahead of time. Having stories you are ready to tell will allow you to focus on listening to the interviewer – not thinking about what you are going to say while they are still speaking. This will allow you to better tailor your answers to the question.

Lesson 9 Exercises

In lesson 8, you were asked to develop three STAR(L) stories. Review your stories and ensure that they:

- *Clearly define the situation*

- *Follow a clear sequence of actions that are easy to follow*

- *Provide specific results that are related to expectations for the position that you identified in Lesson 3*

If your answer accomplishes these three things, it should be a pretty good answer. Exceptional answers incorporate two additional items:

- *Thoughts: What were your thoughts and concerns when you first encountered the situation in your story?*

- *Lessons Learned: What did you take away from the experience that will make you more effective in the future?*

The STAR(L) may be the most powerful interview technique in this book. If you work on nothing else, make sure you master Lessons 8 & 9.

Lesson 10
Experience Questions

Questions about your experience should be easy. Unfortunately, many job seekers find the task of remembering details from five, ten or more years ago is not as easy as it seems.

Many job seekers have experienced this pitfall. They are asked a question about something that was an integral element of their daily routine for years. Their initial thought is "This is easy. I did that all the time." Then they start to answer and the words are not there. They know the memory is in there but cannot recall all the specifics quickly. Then they wonder, "How could I have forgotten that? I used to do that all the time."

If you have run into this pitfall, you know it is frustrating and can kill an interview. Forgetting one detail will not doom you, but losing your confidence and panicking will.

Avoiding this is one of the advantages of preparing STAR(L) answers. Scripting out stories of specific actions and accomplishments will help you recall major details from your background. There is still a chance that you will be asked something obscure that you will not be able to remember, but the odds are now lower. Additionally, your confidence should be higher because you know you are prepared and any curves thrown your way will not seem as significant.

The exercises from Lessons 8 and 9 were to prepare three STAR(L) stories related to your effectiveness.

The key to using these stories successfully is being able to customize them in response to a wide range of questions.

In the example from Lesson 6, the STAR(L) was:

- **Situation**: Manage the rollout of a new product
- **Thoughts:** Worried about staying organized
- **Actions:** Met with key players to get buy-in. Planned project and schedule. Held team accountable to the schedule
- **Results:** Completed roll-out 1 week ahead of schedule
- **Lessons Learned:** Learned project management techniques

Now, let us look at some experience questions.

- Describe your leadership style.
- When have you had to lead a team of people that did not report to you?
- How have you helped grow revenues for your employer?

- What did your company expect from you in your last job?

- What major challenges and problems did you face in your last job?

- What is your greatest professional accomplishment?

- Describe the worst boss you have ever had.

- Tell me about a time when you participated on a team. What was your role?

These questions are vastly different, and yet, you can use the STAR(L) method to answer all of them. In fact, you could tailor the example answer from Lesson 9 to answer most of these questions.

A good way to remember details from your experience is to review the performance measures for each position you held. Outline the critical aspects of each job, what you did to meet those demands and the results you achieved. If you take the time to work through this, it is less likely that you will get stumped in an interview. Also, save your notes – it will speed up your prep during future job searches.

Confidentiality

With experience questions, you will be asked about details of your previous jobs and the work you did. Providing answers to most of these questions is expected and routine. There are, however, exceptions.

Many companies have trade secrets that they expect to be kept confidential. If this is the case, you were likely asked to sign a confidentiality agreement governing these trade secrets. You should never violate this agreement.

If a company asks a question about a confidential topic, you should decline to answer and explain that you have a confidentiality agreement preventing you from providing more detail.

There will be interviewers who push you to answer anyway. There are typically two reasons for this. First, they could be hoping you will reveal a trade secret they can use. Second, they could be testing your character to see if they can trust you to maintain their own trade secrets. In either case, providing confidential details will not help you land the job. More likely, you will be eliminated as a candidate because you answered.

Lesson 10 Exercises

Answer the following questions with one of the stories you scripted yesterday.

- Describe your leadership style.
- When have you had to lead a team of people that did not report to you?
- How have you helped grow revenues for your employer?
- What did your company expect from you in your last job?
- What major challenges and problems did you face in your last job?
- What is your greatest professional accomplishment?
- Describe the worst boss you have ever had.
- Tell me about a time when you participated on a team. What was your role?

Write two additional STAR(L) stories that relate to the questions above.

Lesson 11
Skills Questions

Every job has skills that are essential for success. In Lesson 3, you should have prepared a list of the most important skills to the position you are seeking. It is likely that you will be asked to discuss your proficiency with these key skills in an interview. In technical positions, your technical skills may be the focal point of the interview.

The key to making the best impression is showing the interviewer your skill level instead of simply telling them about it. This requires demonstrating the skill.

> Consider pursuing certifications in your field that will objectively demonstrate your skill level. Getting certified can differentiate you from other candidates.

A good way to do this is with the STAR(L) method. Using STAR(L), you can state your skill level and proceed to give an example that demonstrates this skill level.

For example, imagine being asked to assess your skill level with Excel. Most job seekers will state their skill level. Then they describe their ability by saying something about being proficient, very experienced, or an expert. Although this answers the question, it really does not promote your potential. The problem is that the interviewer needs to trust that you are honest, that you have accurately assessed your skills and that the terminology you use means the same thing to you as it does to them. This last point is the real stumbling block. What constitutes being proficient or an expert is not a universally accepted standard.

Adding an example that shows the interviewer your skill level will overcome this. Again, imagine being asked to assess your skill level with Excel. This time, you give a solid example of your experience to support your assessment:

> *I consider myself proficient with Excel. I have worked with Excel for more than five years and use it on a regular basis. As an example, I created a workbook to track our department's budget. This workbook had a number of spreadsheets linked together, with numerous financial formulas and several graphs I used to report monthly results. I also wrote a couple of macros that I used to import data into the workbook from our accounting system. I'm very comfortable working with large sets of data in Excel, using complicated formulas and writing simple macros.*

After an answer like this, the interviewer should have a clear idea of your capability. The answer touches on several different aspects of using Excel. It also opens the door for follow up questions. If writing macros is important to the company, a question about the macros would easily clarify this.

The most important aspect of answering a skills question with an example is its effect on your credibility. Just stating your skills level does nothing to establish trust in your assessment. If you give your personal assessment and back it up with an example, you validate your assessment.

Lesson 11 Exercises

Write two additional STAR(L) stories that demonstrate one or more technical skills that you identified in Lesson 3 as critical to the position you are seeking. The key is to show an interviewer what you have done with the skill, rather than just say you are good with the skill.

Lesson 12
Communication Skills

Communication skills are important in every field. They may be the key requirement or an important secondary element. In either case, they are crucial, and you need to be prepared to demonstrate your ability to communicate effectively.

Communication skills include your speaking skills, presentation skills and writing skills. They also include your ability to persuade and motivate others.

Most job seekers struggle with differentiating their communication skills from those of other job seekers. Almost every job seeker will claim to have good communication skills. Some may admit that their writing skills are weaker than their speaking skills, but pretty much everyone will say they communicate effectively. So, how are you different?

The key is showing the interviewer how you successfully communicated in difficult situations in the past. The STAR(L) stories you were asked to write in Lesson 11 will accomplish this for you.

> Even if you are not asked about your communications skills, your ability to communicate effectively will be assessed. The entire interview is an assessment of your ability to communicate. Many people struggle with public speaking – it is one of the most common phobias. Consider joining a group where you will have the opportunity to practice your public speaking. Toastmasters is one great organization where you can improve communications skills.

Some communication questions you might hear are:

- Tell me about a time when you had to persuade someone quickly.
- Tell me about the most difficult audience you have ever had to face.
- Tell me about a time when you made a presentation.
- Please describe an important written document you were required to complete.
- Tell me about a time when you motivated a team or individual.
- Tell me about a time when you had to communicate an unpopular message.
- Tell me what you would say if your boss told you something you knew to be wrong.
- Tell me about a time that you communicated technical information to a non-technical audience.
- What is your preferred way to communicate - instant message, phone, or email?

Lesson 12 Exercises

Write two STAR(L) stories that relate directly to your communications skills. Your communication skills are extremely important and will be assessed in every interview, regardless of your field.

The stories should focus on one of the following:

- *Your ability to deliver a tough or unpopular message*
- *Your ability to motivate others*
- *Your ability to improve a team's performance through improved communications*

If your STAR(L) hits on these areas, it will not only demonstrate your ability to communicate effectively, it will also demonstrate that your communications skills provide significant value to your employer.

Lesson 13
Career Goals

Many interviewers will ask specific questions about your goals and objectives. They ask these questions for a number of reasons. Your answer can provide a sense of your maturity, motivations or values. The interviewer will also learn how realistic your expectations are. Finally, they will assess how likely you are to accept an offer and gauge how long you are likely to stay if you are hired.

Turnover is extremely costly and companies want to minimize the loss of successful employees. This makes it important to try to satisfy the goals and expectations of employees. The first step is to find out what those expectations are.

If a job seeker has an expectation that they consider extremely important but the interviewer knows will not be satisfied, the interviewer is likely to reject the candidate. The rationale is that the hiring manager may be able to get the job seeker to join the company, but they will not stay long. Hiring managers may pass on a strong candidate if they do not expect the person to stay, and may even select a less qualified candidate that they expect will stay longer.

Fear of turnover is the primary reason over qualified job seekers are rejected. The company assumes the candidate will continue to look for a job after they are hired, since the job is not their ideal fit.

The first step in fielding these questions is to know what you want to do. You need to have a specific goal. You also need to have a plan for your progression. This does not mean that you have to stick with your plan and make it completely inflexible. You can change your plan, and should change it, as you progress in your career. The key is to know what you want.

Although the company will want to know your expectations and goals, their priority is not satisfying your needs. Employers are concerned about their own goals. Be prepared to discuss your goals, but limit the discussion to the questions you are asked. Stay focused on selling your potential. An easy way to kill an opportunity is to get turned around so you are focused on your goals, wants and needs.

There are seven major areas you need to consider in order to assess your goals:

1. Work Environment

The work environment you choose can have a huge effect on the enjoyment of your new career. Some of the alternatives are:

- Do you want to work indoors or outdoors?

- Do you prefer working in a production plant/factory or in an office?
- Do you want to sit at a desk most of the time or be more active?
- Do you want to be in one location or do you want to travel?
- Do you want a high-tech or low-tech environment?

2. Work Schedule

- Do you want a 9-5, five-day-per-week schedule or are your comfortable working more?
- Do you want a set schedule or flexibility in setting your schedule?
- Are you comfortable working a 2nd or 3rd shift?
- Are you willing to work weekends?

3. Company Culture

- Do you want to work on a team or do you prefer working alone?
- Do you want a competitive or cooperative environment?
- Is it important to have your compensation tied to individual performance?
- Do you want a professional or more relaxed culture?

4. Responsibilities

- Do you want a technical position?

- Do you want to function as an individual contributor, team member, team leader, function manager or multi-function manager?

- Do you want administrative responsibilities?

- Are you comfortable working in a sales or business development role?

- Do you work best when left entirely on your own, with loose supervision or when closely managed?

- How would you prefer your performance to be measured; day-to-day informal coaching and feedback, monthly or quarterly "sit-down" reviews, a formal performance review or a comprehensive "three-sixty" review?

5. Location

Where you want to live will dramatically affect the opportunities available to you. The more tightly you define the location you want, the less likely it is that you will find an acceptable opportunity. Define what is ideal for you and what you would accept.

6. Compensation

You need to have an idea of the salary range you are seeking. This is last in our list of important factors because it usually can only be determined once you know the details of a position. When setting your goals for compensation, define a range first. Consider what is the least you would accept up to a level where you would be very happy. The more realistic you are with your goals, the more likely you will find something that meets those goals. This does not mean that you sell yourself short. It just means that if the range of salaries in the marketplace is $60-70K for a position, and you set a goal above $80K, then it is going to be difficult for you to achieve your goal.

Additionally, you will probably have to be much more flexible on the first five factors listed in order to maximize the compensation you receive.

7. Progression

- How long do you want to stay in the job you are seeking?
- What position do you want for your next step?
- What skills and experiences do you want to gain?

Each of these areas is individually important. Together they make up your ideal opportunity.

Lesson 13 Exercises

Review each of the seven career goals listed previously. Write down your expectations for each. Mark the expectations that are requirements for you and which are more flexible.

Category	Minimum Acceptable	Desired Target	Ideal
Work Environment			
Work Schedule			
Company Culture			
Job Responsibilities			
Location			
Compensation			
Progression			

After completing your goals assessment, answer the following questions:

- *What are you looking for in your next job?*
- *Where do you see yourself in five years?*
- *How do you plan to achieve those goals?*
- *Describe the typical workweek you desire.*
- *Do you take work home with you?*
- *How many hours do you normally work?*
- *How do you handle stress and pressure?*
- *What motivates you?*
- *Do you prefer to work independently or on a team?*
- *What type of work environment do you prefer?*
- *Describe your dream job.*
- *Describe a job that would be your worst nightmare.*

Lesson 14
Behavior Based Questions

An increasingly common interview style is the behavior based interview. The premise underlying behavior based interviewing is that past behavior is the most reliable predictor of future performance. With this interview, interviewers attempt to assess candidates based on how they behaved in a variety of circumstances.

The rationale is to determine how an individual would perform by assessing how they have performed in similar situations in the past.

To interview effectively in a behavior based interview, job seekers need to be able to discuss, very specifically, what they have done. The most effective method of preparing is to develop a selection of stories that you can adapt in response to any question.

> It is essential to show what you have done and what you have achieved in answering behavior based questions. If you do not show results then the assumption will be that you did not succeed. The interviewer will only assess the information you provide them. No matter how successful you were, if you cannot provide a clear, specific example with results, you will not be assessed as a success.

Behavior based questions typically follow the "Tell about a time when you..." format. Each question will address one or more attributes that are important for the job. The questions help the interviewer determine how you measure up with the attributes they want.

Many firms that utilize behavior based interviews will use the same or similar questions with every candidate. They do this to make it much easier to compare candidates.

To be successful, it is important to have clear, concise and organized answers. Having interviewed a large number of job seekers, we have seen numerous individuals give answers that are difficult to follow. This makes a very poor impression. Another important factor is having a good grasp of your strengths and weaknesses. Many job seekers have difficulty assessing themselves and even more trouble communicating their assessment. If you want to make a positive impression, knowing what makes you attractive to an employer is critical.

Remember, you are competing against job seekers that have a similar background and the same level of experience (and perhaps more experience). The fact that the employer believes you can do the job got you the interview. To land the job, you need to stand out.

Lesson 14 Exercises

You should have nine STAR(L) stories from Lessons 8, 10, 11 and 12. Utilize these stories to answer the following questions:

- *Describe a difficult work situation and explain how you overcame it.*
- *Describe a time when your workload was heavy.*
- *Tell me about a time when you had to deal with a co-worker who was not doing his/her fair share of the work. What did you do and what was the outcome?*
- *Give me an example of when you took the time to share a co-worker's or supervisor's achievements with others?*
- *Tell me about a time where you did not work well with a supervisor.*
- *Tell me about a time when you misjudged a person.*
- *Tell me about how you worked effectively under pressure.*

The more you practice, the better you will get. At a minimum, answer each question above once, picking the STAR(L) story that best suits each question. Time permitting, try to answer the questions using different stories. This will help you improve your ability to tailor the stories to whatever question you are asked.

Lesson 15
Company and Industry Knowledge

You are expected to research a company and industry before interviewing with them. Some interviewers will test this type of preparation by asking questions on topics they feel you should know. These questions can be specific or open-ended.

The first place to start in researching a company is to go to the company's website. Review the home page and the About Us section. Get a feel for the products and services the company offers. Most company websites will have a page with recent press releases. This is a great way to learn about the direction of the company. Public companies usually have an investor information page where you can learn key financial data on the company.

Once you have reviewed the company website, look for articles written about the company. This can be easily done on Google News or Yahoo News.

Researching a few key competitors can help you get a feel for the company in the context of its industry peers. Look up the websites of two or three competitors. Review the Mission Statements from each and contrast them with the company. Examine the products and services offered by each competitor to see how they position themselves differently. Finally, consider the overall style of each website and how they differ. This can help point out the differences between the corporate cultures.

Be careful with the sources of information you obtain. There are numerous discussion forums where you can read stories from past employees. This information is anecdotal and is not always reliable. Even a factually true story of one employee at a large company may not be representative of the entire company. Additionally, the posting may not tell the whole story. Worse, it may be a complete fabrication. An example is the CEO who posted anonymous false statements about a competitor, stating that the competitor was on the verge of bankruptcy. This drove the competitor's stock price down. The CEO later orchestrated a takeover of the competitor. If you had read the forum posts and believed them, you would have formed an incorrect financial picture of the competitor.

Lesson 15 Exercises

Select your target company. Research the company and answer the following questions:

- *Company Name and Website*

- *How big is the company? (find out the number of employees, total revenues or number of locations)*

- *What are the primary products or services provided by the company?*

- *What is the company's mission statement?*

- *What was the topic of the most recent press release issued by the company?*

- *What are the names of three direct competitors of the company?*

- *What are the mission statements of these competitors?*

- *What was the topic of the most recent press release issued by each competitor?*

_____

_____

_____

_____

_____

With this information, you should be able to field most questions during an interview. This will also help you develop questions to ask in an interview. We will cover questions you should ask in detail in Lesson 19.

Repeat this exercise each time you prepare to interview with a company.

Lesson 16
Career Progression

Most interviewers will ask for details of why you made specific career changes. At the very least, they will want to know why you are changing positions now. Many will want to know why you left your last two or three positions.

You need to be prepared to discuss specifically and honestly the career changes you have made. Interviewers want to know what motivates you and how you performed in previous roles. Your career progression is one the best ways an interviewer can learn about these two areas of interest.

Questions about your progression will focus on why you pursued and accepted each position, and why you left each job. You need to be able to discuss your start and end at each job in detail.

Your progression can be a big selling point to an employer. The times when you were promoted or given additional responsibilities are indications of your success. This is similar to an objective recommendation – the company would not have promoted you if you were not successful.

Your motivators can also create a strong impression. Do you only care about your salary and change jobs at the drop of a hat? Do you have expectations the company can meet? The interviewer wants to select a candidate that will be successful and stay in a job. If you create the impression of not intending to stay in a position, you are more likely to be rejected.

Addressing your career changes is especially important if you left a previous position on unfavorable terms. The truth is many job seekers have been fired at some point in their careers. Be prepared to discuss the reasons you left each position and be honest about the circumstances.

"I was fired."

If your company terminated your employment, it is best not to hide this fact. Most companies will uncover this during their reference checks. If you hide it and it comes out later, you will likely be eliminated from consideration. The company will see it as an attempt to lie or deceive. Worse, if you are hired, and it's uncovered later, you may be fired for lying about it.

How can you discuss this honestly and not get rejected? The key is to be honest. Explain the circumstances under which your former employer chose to terminate your employment.

Discuss what you could have done differently. Most importantly, make your case for why the reason you were fired will not hurt your performance in the future. Did you change careers and move into a field for which you are better suited? Did you have an attendance problem due to something in your personal life that you have since been able to change? Did you lack experience that you have since gained through additional education or another job?

The key is to show why you will be successful in the future. Your first job after being fired will be the toughest to secure. Once you have proven that the previous termination was an anomaly, it will become easier to change positions.

> Losing a job can be very traumatic. It is one of the biggest causes of stress and depression. For some job seekers, getting fired destroys their self-confidence. Your attitude and confidence play a big role in your interview effectiveness. Focus on your past successes. If you become depressed, seek help. This is important for both your personal life and your ability to interview confidently.

"I had the opportunity to gain additional experience"

Many people find their careers stagnate once they are in a position for a lengthy period of time. You may have changed jobs in the past to acquire a new skill. If you are prepared, this can be a great talking point in an interview.

Discuss what you gained in your previous position and the goals you had at the time. Then discuss how your next position helped you gain skills or experiences relevant to your overall career goals and unavailable in your prior position. To make this discussion a winner, make sure you can explain what you learned specifically.

"I hated my job"

There are times when people take jobs that are a poor match for them. Leaving a position you hate for one you love is a positive career move. It is important to be prepared to discuss this in an interview.

Be ready to explain what aspects of the job were not a fit. It is also important to discuss what differences would make a new position a better fit.

There is some risk to giving this answer. You might describe aspects of the position you hated that match the position the company is trying to fill. If this is the case, the hiring manager will probably eliminate you from consideration. Although your first reaction may be to try to avoid this, it may not be a bad thing ultimately.

If you are honest and specific, then you will be describing the type of position you will hate. If the position matches this, then it is not a position you should pursue. You are better off discovering this early in the process.

There are numerous reasons for why you might make a career change – far too many to detail here. Make sure you prepare to discuss each career move you made. Why did you leave? Why was your next position attractive? Why is the current opportunity attractive to you?

You also need to be able to discuss your overall career goals. In what direction are you driving your career? What would you like the next step in your career to be after this? There are no right answers to these questions – they are simply your preferences. What is important, is having a clear, easy to explain response.

Lesson 16 Exercises

For each of your last five positions, answer the following questions:

- *What attracted you to the company?*
- *What attracted you to the job?*
- *What did you expect before you started?*
- *What did you find was different from these expectations?*
- *What could you have done during the interview process to build more realistic expectations?*
- *What aspects of the position did you dislike?*
- *What did you do to improve the situation?*
- *What could you have done differently in that role?*
- *Why did you decide to leave?*
- *What are you looking for in your next position that will be an improvement over your past roles?*

Write down your career goals for the next five years. What position do you want today? What position do you want to move into after that?

Lesson 17
Education

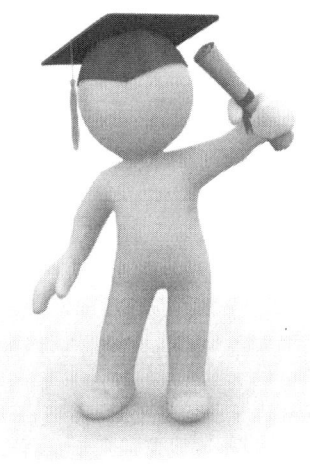

You can expect both formal and informal questions about your education. Recent college graduates will see more of these questions. Three primary types of questions you should expect include:

Formal Education: You could be asked about specific details of your formal education. What classes did you take? What was your GPA? How did you do in the core classes of your major?

Motivation: You could be asked about your motivation for why you pursued the degree(s) you have and what is it about your education you liked and disliked. These questions are more likely to be asked if your education is unrelated to the career you are pursuing.

Continuing Education: You could be asked about your continuing education and professional development. Many companies look for individuals that have a passion for their career and are working to get better. They do not want someone that stopped learning when they got out of school. You should be able to discuss the professional development activities you have conducted in the last year or two. You should also be able to discuss why you are more productive today as compared to a year ago.

Recent Graduates

Recent college graduates often have little to no work experience. Interviews of these individuals focus on their education more than other factors. Without experience, a company will hire you for your potential and ability to learn. Your attitude, work ethic, values and aptitude will be critical elements as you are assessed.

Becoming a Commodity: Many new graduates rely on their degree exclusively. They list the school, major and GPA, expecting these details to secure a job. Your competition will have the same background - a similar school, degree and GPA. If you offer nothing different from everyone else, you become a commodity. To improve your chances, show what makes you different from your competition.

Be able to discuss your study habits. How hard did you work and how did you organize your efforts? Showing your organizational skills can help set you apart from your competition.

In discussing your education, you should also demonstrate your pattern of success. Develop specific examples of when you exceeded the basic requirements of a class. Many classes assign projects with broad guidelines. This offers the opportunity to expand on the assignment and do more than the minimum expectation. Be prepared to discuss, in detail, projects where you exceeded expectations. You want to show your motivation and how this led you to push beyond what was expected.

Lesson 17 Exercises

- *List the continuing education classes you have completed in the last five years*

_____

_____

_____

_____

_____

- *List new skills you have gained in the last two or three years*

_____

_____

_____

_____

_____

- *List ways you stay current on developments in your industry*

_____

_____

_____

_____

_____

Lesson 18
Aptitude

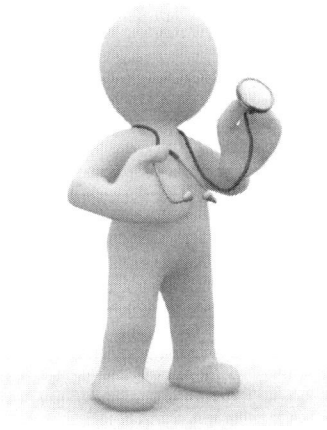

Some interviewers will ask questions designed to test your aptitude and reasoning ability. Usually, you will see this in the form of an assessment test, but it may also be addressed in the interview.

Preparing for questions like this is a challenge, since there is no way to predict what questions will be asked. Keep in mind that the questions are designed to assess your reasoning ability, or the process you use to arrive at the answer, not just the final answer. How you arrive at the answer can be more important than the answer itself.

This type of interview is rare in most fields. There are a few industries where it is more common. Microsoft is a well-known aptitude interviewer. Other tech companies utilize similar interviewing strategies. Consulting firms, think tanks and other organizations that rely on strategic thinking have also commonly used this type of interview question.

How do you prepare? It is impossible to boost your actual aptitude overnight. What you can do is practice a variety of questions in the same style. Practicing will help you pick up some strategies for answering questions and will also put you more at ease when you get an aptitude question. Being confident and relaxed can play a very important role in your ability to impress and interview. If you panic and rush your answer, you will not make as good of an impression.

To find questions to practice, search the Internet for "aptitude test" or for "Microsoft interview." There are websites dedicated to helping job seekers prepare for an interview with Microsoft. Some of these have lengthy lists of questions.

My favorite aptitude question:

> *How many ping pong balls can you put on a Boeing 747?*

In some fields, aptitude tests are common. These range from short quizzes to lengthy assessments that can take hours to complete. If you learn that an assessment test is part of the process, spend some time taking a variety of tests online. Test taking is a skill that can become rusty. A few hours of practice can make a huge difference.

Lesson 18 Exercises

Find an aptitude test online and take it. On completion, assess how comfortable you were taking the test. If you found it awkward and challenging, take additional tests to get more comfortable.

One service that provides affordable assessment testing that job seekers can use to self-test is <u>www.brainbench.com</u>.

There are free assessment tests available. The key is to find a test that simulates the type of aptitude tests or questions you will encounter in your field.

Lesson 19
Creative

Highly creative fields may focus the interview on assessing your creative ability and talents. They also test whether you rattle easily and can adapt to very unpredictable situations.

Some questions designed to assess your creativity are straightforward. They are similar to other skills based questions. For Example,

- Are you creative?
- When have done something innovative?
- What is the most creative thing you have ever done?
- Would you prefer a routine or creative career?

If you have prepared STAR(L) stories for a wide variety of accomplishments in your career, these should be easy.

There is another category of creative questions that are much more difficult to anticipate. These are the "off the wall" questions. They are designed to be completely unexpected.

Perhaps the best known of these is the "If you were a tree, what kind of tree would you be?" It is not a question that has a right answer. It is also not something most people have thought about. Other questions like this include:

- If you could dine with anyone from history, who would it be?
- If you were a fictional character, who would you be?
- If you were a superhero, what would your super powers be?

The key to preparing for questions like this is to stay relaxed.

Take your time answering questions. Many people get nervous in an interview and rush to answer. They feel like every second of silence is an eternity and start answering immediately. The interviewer usually has a different perception. A two or three second lull is just that, a few seconds of silence. If you get a question that is a complete surprise, take a couple of seconds to think before you begin to answer.

Lesson 19 Exercises

Go hug a tree. Try to imagine your inner tree. What kind of tree are you?

OK. You do not really have to hug a tree, but think about a few of the questions above. If you were asked one of these in an interview, how would you react? Would you panic? Would you be irreverent? Would you calmly assess the question and answer it?

If you think these questions might rattle you, answer a few of them until you feel comfortable.

Does your industry commonly ask these types of questions? If so, you should do some research on the largest companies in your field. There are probably individuals that have written about the questions these companies ask in their interviews. For example, both Microsoft and Google are the objects of entire websites dedicated to their hiring process.

Lesson 20
Compensation

At some point in the interview process, the discussion of money, benefits and other compensation factors will come up. Many job seekers are uncomfortable discussing money. Some fear they will sell themselves short. Others worry that they will appear greedy. Most worry about both.

The first step in preparing for a discussion about money is to know what you need and want. In Lesson 10, we covered the goal setting process. You should have a clear idea of what an acceptable compensation level is for you.

It is usually not a good idea to initiate a discussion about compensation. Let the interviewer raise the topic. When asked, you have two options. First, you can decline to answer and simply state you are flexible and just want to be fairly compensated. Second, you can answer honestly with what you want.

> Salary Creep: We have watched a number of candidates "give themselves a raise" during the interview process. As the person progresses through the interviews, they are complimented repeatedly. This is routine with many interviewers, and often is just the interviewer being polite. Despite this, some job seekers will assume the company must really want them and is willing to pay more to get them. The job seeker then raises the level of compensation expected. If you are given a target or range of compensation at the start of the process, it is unlikely that it will increase over the course of the selection process. Work to maintain realistic expectations.

If you choose the first option and decline to give a specific answer, there is a good chance the interviewer will ask a follow up question, requesting you to be specific. If this happens, do not fight the interviewer. Tell them what you want.

Be careful not to get too picky. Your overall compensation is what is important. One company may offer a moderate salary and great benefits. Another might offer a great salary and have very limited benefits. If you require a specific salary level, you may exclude yourself from consideration for the position with great benefits, when the overall compensation would be acceptable. The key is to know what you need and wait to see the total compensation package the company offers.

Lesson 20 Exercises

Review your goals from Lesson 10. What is the minimum compensation you would accept for an ideal opportunity?

Review salaries for the position you are seeking. You can do this at websites like www.salary.com. Are your expectations in line with the marketplace?

Lesson 21
Off Limits Questions

There are a variety of questions interviewers should not ask. These questions are off limits because they provide information that can be used to discriminate illegally. As a general rule, questions that do not relate to an aspect of the job seeker's ability to perform the essential functions of the job should be avoided.

The categories of questions that are considered off limits include:

- Applicant's race or color
- Applicant's age
- Applicant's sexual orientation
- Applicant's national origin
- Applicant's marital status
- Applicant's religion
- Applicant's citizenship
- Applicant's maiden name

- Applicant's medical status
- Military discharge (type, when received)
- Arrest record (note: employers can't ask about an arrest, but they may ask about convictions)

Any question designed to help the employer discriminate against someone for a reason unrelated to their ability to perform the job is off limits. This can include wide variety of personal details.

If you are asked a question that touches on one of these areas, the best strategy is usually to try to avoid answering. You may decline to answer as the question relates to something personal and you feel it is private.

There are a few very limited situations where the off limits questions may become acceptable. For example, a church hiring a religious education instructor may have justification for asking an applicant about their religious beliefs (although if you are hiring in this situation – talk to an employment attorney to be certain). Generally, questions about the topics listed above do not relate to the ability of a job seeker to perform the job.

Anti-discrimination laws and the guidelines for acceptable interview questions vary greatly around the world. In some countries, questions about family status, age or other personal details are routine and are considered acceptable. If you are interviewing for an international position, be prepared for differences in the assessment process.

Lesson 22
Your Questions

The conclusion of the interview will give you the chance to ask questions. This is an important part of the interview. You should have questions. At the very least, you should be assessing the company to determine if it is the right fit for you. You can also learn more about the future of the company.

Assessing Fit

You will want to learn as much about the culture of the company as you can. Asking questions about how employees work together and interact can shed light on the company's culture. You can also clarify details of the role, asking about specific responsibilities or challenges.

The Future of the Company

In Lesson 15, we reviewed strategies for researching a potential employer. Information from the company's mission statement and recent press releases can help you understand the values and direction of the company. You can ask questions to clarify the values and direction.

Greatest Challenge

If the hiring manager does not share the greatest challenge of the position, you should ask about it. This will help you understand the core problem the hiring manager wants to solve. It also gives you the opportunity to respond with how your experience can solve that problem or how you have solved similar problems in the past.

Biggest Obstacle

If you are worried the interviewer is not convinced you are the right fit, and you are not told why, you can open this up for discussion. The following question is a good way to get started:

"Is there anything about my background or experience that you feel might make it challenging for me to succeed in this role?"

If the interviewer does have a concern, they often will share it. You then have the opportunity to respond to the concern. You will not change their opinion every time, but you will give yourself a chance. If you leave the interview with a major concern in the interviewer's mind, it is unlikely you will be selected.

> Stick with questions about topics you want answered. The impression you make with your questions is only one factor. If you develop questions solely for the purpose of impressing the interviewer, this will show.

At a minimum, you should have five questions you are prepared to ask. Some questions can be asked in multiple interviews. This can give an interesting perspective of how different managers see the same company.

It is best to choose questions tailored to the company and the position. There are a number of more generic questions that are also good to ask. For example:

- Why is this position open?

- How will I be assessed and my performance measured in this role?

- How often will I be assessed and by whom?

- What characteristics do you most value in an employee?

- What does a person in this position need to accomplish to be considered successful?

Lesson 22 Exercises

List five questions that you have about the company or position you are pursuing based on the research you did in Lesson 12.

1. _____

   _____

2. _____

   _____

3. _____

   _____

4. _____

   _____

5. _____

   _____

Lesson 23
Mock Interviews

We have now finished preparing answers for different types of questions. The next step is working on the delivery. Very few job seekers practice their interview skills. They prepare a few answers and head off to the interview, sure that they are an expert about themselves.

Unfortunately, knowing about your background and preparing answers in advanced is not enough. Writing the answer to a question is vastly different from having to adapt to a question you did not expect. Rehearse your answers repeatedly. Get comfortable with describing important aspects of your background. The goal is to get sufficiently comfortable to adapt your answers to each question and have them sound professional and unscripted.

Mock interviews are a great way to prepare. Simulating a real interview allows you to practice different ways of phrasing things.

The feedback from mock interviewers is also very beneficial. You will find out if you are saying something that is interpreted incorrectly. You may be inadvertently hurting your chances and not know it.

A good Mock Interview will have the following elements:

- **Unexpected Questions:** The questions asked in the mock interview should not be prepared by you. Part of simulating a real interview is the uncertainty of what you will be asked. Ask the interviewer to prepare the list of questions.

- **Unfamiliar Interviewer:** A real interview will usually be with someone you do not know. Getting a family member or friend to conduct the mock interview cannot simulate this adequately. Work to find someone that you do not know well. The interviewer should take you out of your comfort zone. The more you can simulate the stress of a real interview, the greater the benefit you will get from the mock interview.

- **A Skilled Interviewer:** It is important that the individual conducting the mock interview is skilled and experienced at interviewing. They need to be able to compare your interview to others they have conducted to properly assess you.

- **Uninterrupted Environment:** Make sure the location of your mock interview is free from distractions. You want to focus on the interview the same way you would if it was a real interview.

If your mock interview is conducted by phone, you can easily record the call to review your performance. Skype has a plug-in application (Pamela) that makes recording a call very easy. Just make sure you follow any applicable laws on recorded calls.

- **Honest Feedback:** The interviewer should feel comfortable providing honest and critical feedback. You do not want to receive feedback from someone afraid of hurting your feelings. That will not help. You want someone that will be as critical as a hiring manager would be in a real interview.

During a mock interview, we keep a watch or clock in our line of sight during the interview. We then write down the time (minutes and seconds) each time we ask a question. This allows us to check the duration of each answer. Most answers should be two to three minutes long. Shorter than this and you may not provide enough detail; longer than this, you may lose the interviewer.

Lesson 23 Exercises

Conduct a mock interview with an interviewer who is experienced in interviewing and assessing job seekers. Let the interviewer select the questions – do not give the interviewer a script – it is important to practice adapting to unexpected questions.

Ask the interviewer to assess each of your answers for the following:

- *Were you confident?*
- *Were you enthusiastic?*
- *Did you use many filler words (Um, Ah, or other sounds)?*
- *Did you use any jargon the interviewer might not understand?*
- *Did you provide a substantive accomplishment, clearly detailing the situation, actions and results achieved?*
- *Did you relate your answer to the specific expectations of the opportunity?*
- *Was your answer easy to follow?*
- *Was your answer concise?*
- *Overall, did your answer make a positive, negative or neutral impression?*

At a minimum, conduct one mock interview. Ideally, you should complete two or three mock interviews. At each interview, you will improve your skills and effectiveness.

Lesson 24
Going to Your Interview

As your interview approaches, you will need to do a few final preparatory tasks. The key is to ensure that you can focus on your interview without distractions.

First, make sure you have directions to the interview. This is something that many people have forgotten, causing them to be late for an interview.

Second, make sure you research the company you are interviewing. It is commonly expected that you will do your homework before an interview. Failing to research a company sends the message that you are not interested, and that you are not thorough. This is not the impression you want to create.

Third, have your Tell Me About Yourself remarks firmly imbedded in your mind. You know you are going to get this question in many interviews. Being prepared helps alleviate any initial nervousness.

Fourth, make sure you are comfortable with the STAR(L) method. You are not going to know what questions are going to be asked but following a logical sequence when using an example to respond to any question, will make you more effective. Practice some responses using this method.

Fifth, gather all the key materials you are going to take to the interview. There are several items you should consider:

- **A folder or portfolio:** A leather or imitation leather portfolio is a very professional accessory. It also allows you to organize the other items you will be carrying.
- **Additional copies of your resume:** Most interviewers will have your resume when you meet, but on the off chance that they do not have it, you should bring several copies. This also helps if your resume has been faxed or copied. Giving a clean copy is a good move here.
- **A notepad:** You should write down the name and title of everyone you meet. Often they will give you a business card with their contact information. Make sure you get enough information to send a follow up letter thanking them for their time.
- **Any other information that the company has requested:** Sometimes companies will ask you to bring a list of references, or application paperwork filled out in advance.

On the day of the interview, make sure you arrive early. Planning to arrive at least 30 minutes early is a good way to ensure that you have time to adjust to any problems—like traffic congestion. Since waiting in a reception area for long periods of time can be awkward, you might want to wait in your car or go to a restaurant nearby.

 Make sure you have a cell phone with you. If you get lost, break down or get stuck in traffic, it is good to have a way to contact the interviewer. Just make sure you either leave the phone in the car or turn it off. You do not want to have your cell phone ring during an interview.

Most importantly on the day of the interview, try to relax. You have already prepared. Now is the time to get focused, while maintaining the confidence you naturally have.

Lesson 25
What to Expect

Each company conducts interviews differently. Some emphasize individual interviews, others prefer group interviews. Knowing what you may run into will help you adapt to a wide range of circumstances.

Settings

Usually, your interview will take place in a private office or in a conference room. This is not always the case though. Some settings you may encounter include:

- **Private Office:** You meet in the interviewer's office
- **Conference Room:** You meet in a conference room or other multi-use room

- **Interview Tour:** The interviewer conducts the interview while giving you a tour of the facility

If you expect a facility tour during your interview, consider the type of facility when deciding how to dress. Many manufacturing facilities will not allow open toed shoes. Some facilities have smooth concrete floors and metal stairs. These can be very slick with leather-soled shoes, especially when new. Consider getting a pair of shoes resoled with a rubber tread. This will make walking around a production facility much easier and safer.

- **Restaurant:** You meet the interviewer at a restaurant for a breakfast, lunch or dinner and are interviewed during the meal. When you have a full day of interviews at a company, there will usually be a lunch interview during the day.

When interviewing over a meal, try to order something simple and easy to eat. You want to concentrate on the interviewer, not the food. Peel and eat shrimp, crab legs and fajitas are too much work. They will distract you from the conversation. Also, avoid foods that are prone to spill, such as spaghetti.

- **Busy Office:** Some interviewers will conduct the interview in an office that has a lot of foot traffic in and out. This can be very distracting. The key is to stay focused and relaxed. Do not let interruptions affect you.

- **Airport:** If the hiring manager travels a lot, they may want to schedule an interview during a layover in your city. This allows them to meet with you early in the process without the complexity and expense of flying you in. Like the Busy Office, do not let the events around you distract you. Stay relaxed.

- **Mass Interview Room:** Companies that hire large numbers of people for the same position may set up an interview room with desks that allow several interviews to be conducted simultaneously. This style is more common with large manufacturing and distribution facilities filling large numbers of entry level positions. Some people find it awkward to be interviewed with another interview going on a few feet away. Do not let this bother you. Usually, a company hiring in this mode has a large number of positions to fill. They may hire everyone that they think is qualified. In this situation, you are not competing against the other job seekers. You only need to demonstrate that you meet the requirements for the position.

- **Neutral Site Interview:** Some hiring managers prefer to interview away from their office. This is more common with small companies. Like the restaurant interview, you may meet in almost any public setting. Starbucks is a popular location for this. We have also seen interviews conducted in hotel lobbies, local parks, picnic areas and shopping malls.

- **In the Car:** This may be the rarest interview location. We know of one situation where a hiring manager was flying to a city for a meeting, but did not have time to schedule a separate meeting for an interview with a candidate. Instead, the candidate picked up the hiring manager at the airport and the interview was conducted during the drive.

What setting should you expect? A private office or conference room is most likely. Some of the settings listed are highly unlikely, but they are possible. If you find that your interview is in a setting that you did not expect, do not let it throw you off your game.

Interviewers

Most interviews are conducted as a one-on-one meeting but there is a wide range of possibilities such as:

- **One-on-One:** You meet with a single interviewer at a time.

- **Paired Interviews:** You meet with two interviewers simultaneously. Often one individual will take the lead and do the majority of the talking.

- **Group Interview:** You may be interviewed by three or more people at a time. Like the paired interview, usually one person will take the lead and ask most of the questions, with the others asking an occasional follow-up question.

> The personality of each interviewer in a paired, group or panel interview will vary. Some may have a friendly style, others may be clinical in their approach. You may even have a confrontational interviewer in the mix. Adapting to different styles can be intimidating. Your first step in this situation is to focus on listening. Make sure you take the time to understand each question. The questions may not follow a consistent progression, jumping from one topic to another. If you focus on understanding each question, you will respond more effectively.

- **Panel Interviews:** In a panel interview, you will meet with a number of people simultaneously. Each will have questions they want to ask. Although one individual may moderate the panel, each interviewer will take the lead in asking questions at some point during the interview.

- **Group Lunch:** When you have a day of interviews and are taken to lunch, it is likely that you will meet with multiple interviewers. In some situations, the company may be interviewing multiple candidates the same day and will take all of the candidates and interviewers to lunch together.

- **In Person and Conference Call:** In a face-to-face interview, the interviewer may set up a conference call so offsite individuals can participate in the call.

- **Video Conference:** When interviewers cannot meet in the same location, a video conference may link two or more locations. All of the interviewers may be offsite or consist of a combination of offsite and onsite interviewers.

There are numerous variations on the interview setting and the people who interview you. Be prepared to adapt to different settings and do not let unusual circumstances affect the quality of your interviewing.

Lesson 26
After the Interview

After your interview, there are a few important things to do. Some of these activities will help get an offer for the position. Other activities will help with different opportunities.

Thank You Notes

It is very important that you send a Thank You note to the interviewers after the interview.

Do this as soon as possible after the conclusion of your interview. Sending a note reinforces your interest in the position and sends a positive signal about you personally. A Thank you note is not necessary after your initial Phone Screen interview.

There are differences of opinion as to whether you should send an email thank you or a letter by mail. There are advantages to both methods. The important thing is to send the thank you.

Information Requests

Some interviews will conclude with a request for specific information. If a company asks for references, a transcript or other information you cannot provide during the interview, work to provide this information as soon as possible after the interview.

Research the Company

You may learn details about the company in the interview that are significant factors in your decision-making process. If this happens, research the details you learned.

Assess Your Performance

Every interview gives you the opportunity to improve your interview skills. To ensure you maximize the benefit of the experience, assess your performance.

Ask yourself these questions:

- Were there any questions that stumped you? Why were you caught off guard?

- What type and style of interview did you have? Were you comfortable with this?

- What follow-up questions were you asked? Often, an interviewer will ask a follow up question because the job seeker either failed to answer the original question or did not provide sufficient detail.

- What questions did you ask? How did you perceive that these questions were received?

- If you go back to the start of the interview, would you do anything different?

Save the answers to these questions. Over time, you will continue to refine and improve your interview skills.

Conclusions

Interviewing is a skill that can have one of the most significant impacts on your career. Poor interview skills will limit your opportunities, and great interview skills will help you maximize your career potential.

If you follow the advice in this book and complete the exercises, you will dramatically improve your potential. You will interview with more confidence and more effectively. Most importantly, you will gain a significant advantage over your competition.

Few activities can have as big an effect on your earning potential. Improving your interview skills can help you beat out other candidates with more experience and a better education.

Fortunately, improving interview skills can be done quickly and by anyone. We have watched job seekers struggle for months in a job search, only to turn things around in a few weeks by working on their interview skills.

You do not need to go back to school and spend a couple of years getting a Master's degree. You are not required to get a new certification, gain a new skill or get years of experience a role. You just need to improve your ability to communicate your potential and the value you will provide.

The lessons in the book are designed to help you improve quickly. We focused on the elements that will have the biggest impact in the shortest time. Following our advice, you will be better prepared than the vast majority of your competition.

Continuous Improvement

No matter how much you improved over the course of this book, the journey is not over. There will always be opportunities to improve your interview skills. Fortunately, working on these skills can be done on a routine basis and have benefits beyond landing a job.

Your interview skills will help in almost every business situation. Whether you are presenting a project proposal to senior management or in a meeting with your boss, being able to market your ideas is essential.

The STAR(L) can be adapted to a wide variety of circumstances. The Key is presenting the background of a situation, the actions taken and the results. If you do this, you will communicate effectively and your contributions will be much clearer to those around you.

Your Next Job Search

Ideally, you will only change jobs once every few years. If this is the case, it is likely your interview skills will become stale. Your first interview after years of not interviewing will be much worse than you expect. This is natural. Fortunately, your interview skills are still there – you just need to remember them.

In future, each time you start a new search, work through this book. It will remind you of lessons you have learned and you will quickly get up to speed.

After you have prepared, make sure you do a couple mock interviews. It will only take a couple for you to return to peak form. It is important to practice before your first real interview. You do not want to make a mistake when it counts.

Final Thoughts

When you prepare to interview, you can work on hundreds of questions, answers and concepts to improve your skill and comfort level interviewing. If you try to remember all of these during the interview, you will most likely flounder. There is just too much to worry about.

To be successful, you need to relax during an interview. When you get out of your car and walk into the building where you will be interviewing, forget everything you have prepared. Listen closely to the interviewer and answer the questions naturally. If you have prepared well, you will automatically apply the techniques in this book.

Be yourself. Do not try to act like someone else. Interviewing effectively is not an attempt to sell yourself as something you are not. You will be more genuine and successful if you present a true picture of who you are.

Every interview will be different. No matter how much you prepare, there will always be questions that you did not expect. If you prepared a strong positioning statement, then worked this statement into a good "Tell Me About Yourself" answer and developed a variety of good STAR(L) stories, you will be well ahead of your competition.

Good luck in your next interview!

Appendix
Interview Questions

There are thousands of potential questions you could be asked in an interview. It is impossible to prepare an answer for every individual question. Instead, focus on preparing answers for all of the types of questions you could see. Below is a list of questions mentioned in the book. Review these questions and make sure you are comfortable with all of the topics. If you are comfortable, relaxed and confident, you will make the best impression.

- What have you done that has caused you to stand out among your peers?
- What have you done that ever caused your company to generate income?
- What have you done that ever caused your company to reduce costs?
- What have you done that ever caused your company to save time or to become more efficient?
- Tell Me About Yourself
- Why should I hire you?
- What makes you better than others doing your job?
- Why do you think you will be successful here?
- How many people did you manage and what were your responsibilities?
- Tell me about a time when you faced a difficult leadership challenge.
- Give me a few examples of macros you have written in Excel.
- If you were a tree, what kind of tree would you be?
- Tell me about a time when you had to work under a tight

deadline.
- What accomplishment are you most proud of?
- Tell me about a project you managed.
- What is your greatest strength?
- Describe your leadership style.
- When have you had to lead a team of people that did not report to you?
- How have you helped grow revenues for your employer?
- What did your company expect from you in your last job?
- What major challenges and problems did you face in your last job?
- What is your greatest professional accomplishment?
- Describe the worst boss you have ever had.
- Tell me about a time when you participated on a team. What was your role?
- Tell me about a time when you had to persuade someone quickly.
- Tell me about the most difficult audience you have ever had to face.
- Tell me about a time when you made a presentation.
- Please describe an important written document you were required to complete.
- Tell me about a time when you motivated a team or individual.
- Tell me about a time when you had to communicate an unpopular message.
- Tell me what you would say if your boss told you something you knew to be wrong.
- Tell me about a time that you communicated technical information to a non-technical audience.
- What is your preferred way to communicate - instant message, phone, or email?
- What are you looking for in your next job?
- Where do you see yourself in five years?

- How do you plan to achieve those goals?
- Describe the typical workweek you desire.
- Do you take work home with you?
- How many hours do you normally work?
- How do you handle stress and pressure?
- What motivates you?
- Do you prefer to work independently or on a team?
- What type of work environment do you prefer?
- Describe your dream job.
- Describe a job that would be your worst nightmare
- Describe a difficult work situation and explain how you overcame it.
- Describe a time when your workload was heavy.
- Tell me about a time when you had to deal with a co-worker who was not doing his/her fair share of the work. What did you do and what was the outcome?
- Give me an example of when you took the time to share a co-worker's or supervisor's achievements with others?
- Tell me about a time that you did not work well with a supervisor.
- Tell me about a time that you misjudged a person.
- Tell me about how you worked effectively under pressure.
- How big is the company? (find out the number of employees, total revenues or number of locations)
- What are the primary products or services provided by the company?
- What is the company's mission statement?
- What was the most recent press release issued by the company?
- What are the names of three direct competitors of the company?
- What are the mission statements of these competitors?
- What was the most recent press release issued by each competitor?

- What attracted you to each of your last five positions?
- Why did you leave each of your last five positions?
- What continuing Education classes have you completed recently?
- What new skills have you gained in the last 3 years?
- How do you stay current on developments in your industry?
- How many ping pong balls can you put on a Boeing 747?
- Are you creative?
- When have you done something innovative?
- What is the most creative thing you have ever done?
- Would you prefer a routine or creative career?
- If you have dinner with anyone from history, who would it be?
- If you were a fictional character, who would you be?
- If you were a superhero, what would your super powers be?

Index

B

Brainbench · 89

C

Career Goals · 38, 63, 68, 80, 82
Communication Skills · 60
Communications Skills · 38
Company Culture · 65
Company/Industry Knowledge · 39
Compensation · 66, 93
Continuing Education · 84

D

Discrimination · 96

G

Group Interview · 112

I

Interview Settings · 109
Interview Style
   Clinical · 33
   Confrontational · 34
   Friendly · 33
Interview Types
   Behavior Based · 27, 29, 38, 70
   Creative / Aptitude · 87, 90
   Creative/Aptitude · 28, 29
   Experience Based · 26, 29
   Skill Based · 28, 29, 90
Interviewers · 112

L

Location · 66

M

Microsoft Interview · 88, 92
Mock Interview · 14
Mock Interviews · 102

O

Off Limits Questions · 40, 96
Over Qualified · 64

P

Phone Screen · 5
Positioning Statement · 14, 21, 24, 41
Progression · 67

R

Responsibilities · 65

S

Salary.com · 95
STAR(L) · 42, 52, 57, 61, 62, 72, 91, 107
   Actions · 43, 48
   Example · 46
   Lessons Learned · 43
   Results · 43, 49
   Situation · 43, 48
   Thoughts · 43, 48

T

Technical Skills · 28, 38, 56
Tell Me About Yourself · 10, 11, 22, 23, 24, 37, 41, 107
Thank You Notes · 114

W

Work Environment · 64
Work Schedule · 65

Y

Your Questions · 13, 98

PALLADIAN INTERNATIONAL, LLC

Palladian International is an executive search firm hired by a select group of companies to identify and attract the highest performing individuals and separate them from those of mediocre skills. We specialize in working with manufacturing, distribution, sales, marketing and defense organizations for management and executive level positions. We have successfully completed searches in the North America, Europe and the Middle East.

With our extensive recruiting background, we are experts in assessing job seekers. Knowing that our firm possessed the skills to help candidates market themselves much better, Palladian introduced Palladian Career Resources, our coaching service for individuals.

Palladian Career Resources offers a variety of services and resources to job seekers. We write a daily blog with job search advice, offer free resume writing and interviewing guides. We also offer a suite of coaching services for resume writing and interview coaching.

To learn more about executive recruiting services, go to www.palladianinternational.com

To learn more about our coaching business, go to www.PalladianCR.com

To read our Blog, go to http://blog.PalladianCR.com.

Palladian International, LLC
105-A Lew Dewitt Blvd. Suite 197 ~ Waynesboro, VA 22980
866-766-8447

Made in the USA